SONS

Published by Willow Creek Press, Inc.
P.O. Box 147, Minocqua, Wisconsin 54548

Photo Credits:

p4 © John Hyde/age fotostock; p7 © Alaska Stock/Masterfile; p8 © Jurgen & Christi/FLPA/age fotostock; p11 © Winfried Wisniewski/Minden Pictures; p12 © Lisa & Mike Husar/www.teamhusar.com; p15 © Kevin Elsby/FLPA/Minden Pictures; p16 © J W W Lowman/FLPA/Minden Pictures; p19 © Classic Stock/Masterfile; p23 © Cyril Ruoso/Minden Pictures; p24 © Yva Momatiuk & John Eastcott/Minden Pictures; p27 © Frank Krahmer/Masterfile; p28 © Anup Shah/Minden Pictures; p31 © John Foster/Masterfile; p32 © Steve Gettle/Minden Pictures; p35 © Angelo Gandolfi/Minden Pictures; p36 © Lisa & Mike Husar/www.teamhusar.com; p39 © James Hager/age fotostock; p40 © Curtis R. Lantinga/Masterfile; p43 © Lisa & Mike Husar/www.teamhusar.com; p44 © isselee/Masterfile; p47 © R. Wilken/Blickwinkel/age fotostock; p48 © cynoclub/Masterfile; p51 © Corbis RF/age fotostock; p52 © Lisa & Mike Husar/www.teamhusar.com; p55 © beltsazar/Masterfile; p59 © Michio Hoshino/Minden Pictures; p60 © Thomas Kokta/Masterfile; p63 © Tui De Roy/Minden Pictures; p64 © Theo Allofs/Masterfile; p67 © Tierfotoagentur/J. Hutfluss/age fotostock; p68 © Blend Images/Masterfile; p71 © Radomir Jakubowski/NPL/Minden Pictures; p72 © Kelly Funk/All Canada Photos/age fotostock; p75 © Mitsuaki Iwago/Minden Pictures; p76 © Mark Raycroft/Minden Pictures; p79 © Lisa & Mike Husar/www.teamhusar.com; p80 © Suzi Eszterhas/Minden Pictures; p83 © Bernd Zoller/imageBROKER/age fotostock; p84 © Martin Ruegner/Masterfile; p87 © Arco Images GmbH/Kimball Stock; p88 © Richard Du Toit/Minden Pictures; p91 © Hiroya Minakuchi/Minden Pictures; p92 © F Lukasseck/Masterfile; p95 © Vince Burton/NIS/Minden Pictures; p96 © Roland Seitre/Minden Pictures

Design: Donnie Rubo
Printed in China

SONS

LIFE'S GREATEST PRIDE, WORRY, AND JOY

Bonnie Louise Kuchler

⊡ WILLOW CREEK PRESS®

For my son,
Nate

I have a son,

who is my heart.

~Maya Angelou (1928–2014), American poet and author

When you toddled about, beating your chest,

waving a stick-sword and sputtering Batman noises,

I knew that someday you'd be compelled to

prove yourself, to push past your limits,

to see what you were made of.

Would you drive too fast?

Would you throw the first punch?

Would you serve your country, in harm's way?

When those thoughts came,

I squeezed your pint-sized body tight,

as if a warm hug could freeze time.

Letting go would've been easy if you were made

of Kevlar instead of skin; titanium instead of love.

A little at a time, I learned to feed slack to that tether,

until finally I could lay it down, until I could cherish

moments with you, and cling to memories instead.

Life is all memory except for the one
present moment that goes by you so
quick you hardly catch it going.

~Tennessee Williams (1911-1983), American playwright

One of the best things in the world is to be a boy;

it requires no experience,

but needs some practice to be a good one.

~Charles Dudley Warner (1829-1900), American essayist and novelist

You were three-parts angel, one-part alien,
all parts perfect (when you were sleepin').
One-part mud, one-part springs,
destroyer of rugs and little glass things.
Foot on the pedal of life not-yet-lived,
tank full of gas, muffler defective.
"A boy is a noise with smudges," it's true,
but I wouldn't change one smidgen of you.

My mother had a great deal of trouble with me,
but I think she enjoyed it.

~Mark Twain (1835 -1910), American author and humorist

Childhood is the only time in our lives
when insanity is not only permitted to us
but expected.

———•———

~Louis de Bernières, British novelist

The Force was strong with you.
You were champion of the underdogs,
spying on the enemy from
your hidden rebel base.
All it took was a flashlight-
come-saber, and
you were at once a Jedi,
in a world far, far away.

A boy can swim like a fish, run like a deer,
climb like a squirrel, balk like a mule,
bellow like a bull, eat like a pig,
or act like a jackass
according to climatic conditions.

~Author unknown

You were a cherub
with a crooked grin that made me wonder
what you had hiding under those wings.

Why little boys should drive away

Little sweet maidens from the play,

Or love to banter and fight so well,

That's the thing I could never tell.

———•———

~James Hogg (1770-1835), Scottish poet, novelist and essayist

It seemed hard-wired in you,
that thirst to slay dragons.

The boy is a natural spectator; spectating is his passion.
He watches parades, fires, fights, ball games,
dogs, ice wagons, mud turtles, bumblebees,
automobiles, presidents... with equal fervor.

Some things can only be understood
when you're in a treehouse.

~Dr. SunWolf, American professor

The canvas of the world looked so different
through your curious eyes.
How can that bug flap its wings so fast?
Why is this rock a different color than that one?
Where did all the sand come from?
Where I saw dandelion weeds, you
saw geometry in its petals;
where I saw a gloomy sky, you saw a
black stallion in the clouds;
where I saw a dirty, homeless man,
you saw someone who needed help.

Never outgrow your inner superhero.

~Author unknown

I've learned that you
shouldn't go through life
with a catcher's mitt
on both hands.
You need to be able to
throw something back.

~Maya Angelou (1928-2014),
American poet and author

No person was ever honored for what he received;
honor has been the reward for what he gave.

~Calvin Coolidge (1872-1933), America's 30th president

It doesn't matter to me if you are
artistic or mechanical,
a hairdresser, a warrior,
a comic, or a philosopher.
It matters that you give something of yourself,
and that in those moments you feel gratified.
Whatever trail calls your name,
my heart will proudly come alongside.

Don't laugh at a youth for his affectations;
he is only trying on one face after another
to find a face of his own.

———•———

~Logan Pearsall Smith (1865-1946), American-born British writer

Caring heart or stubborn head–
which would have the strongest pull?
I watched you battle yourself, fiercely,
making hard choices only you could make,
finding the balance that would
define the man you would become.

The greatest conflicts are not between two people
but between one person and himself.

~Garth Brooks, American singer and songwriter

To be yourself in a world
that is constantly trying to make you something else
is the greatest accomplishment.

~Ralph Walda Emerson (1803-1882), American poet and essayist

You filled your pockets with
security and a bit of mischief.
It began with rocks and frogs,
then phones and pocketknives,
then money and keys; but always,
in a pocket tucked close to your heart
you carried your treasure—
a pocketful of kindness.

Boys do not grow up gradually.
They move forward in spurts like the
hands of clocks in railway stations.

——•——

~Cyril Cannally (1903-1974), British writer and editor

There comes a time...

when he has a raging desire to go somewhere

and dig for hidden treasure.

~Mark Twain (1835 -1910), American author and humorist

Success isn't a result of
spontaneous combustion.
You must set yourself on fire.

~Arnold Henry Glasow (1905-1998),
American businessman and humorist

God gives us dreams a size too big

so that we can grow in them.

~Author unknown

It takes an uncommon amount of guts
to put your dreams on the line,
to hold them up and say,
"How good or how bad am I?"
That's where courage comes in.

~Erma Bombeck (1927-1996), American humorist and writer

Courage is resistance to fear, mastery of fear—
not absence of fear.

~Mark Twain (1835-1910), American author and humorist

Bite off more than you can chew,

then chew it.

~Author unknown

You inherited a complicated world—
a world of fragile opportunities,
a Petri dish of anxiety and discontent.
When distraction scatters your energy
and leaves you frustrated,
glue your sights to one goal—
a single goal that means more to you than anything else.
Even crawling will get you there,
if you just keep moving.

There are no shortcuts to any place worth going.

~ Beverly Sills (1929-2007),
American soprano opera performer

Work hard, fight hard, and do the best you can;
Deserve the victory or refuse the prize.
'Tis better far to be the beaten man
Than take the glory and yourself despise.

~Author unknown

Inside of a ring or out,
ain't nothing wrong with going down.
It's staying down that's wrong.

———•———

~Muhammad Ali, American professional boxer

During my 18 years I came to bat almost 10,000 times.
I struck out about 1,700 times and walked maybe 1,800 times.
You figure a ballplayer will average about 500 at bats a season.
That means I played seven years without ever hitting the ball.

———•———

~Mickey Mantle (1931-1995), American major league baseball player

Don't forget to swing hard,

in case you hit the ball.

———•———

~Woodie Held (1932-2009),
American major league baseball player

You had to

find your own footing up a mountain of slippery toeholds;

choose your own battles, your allies, your weapons;

decide for yourself, with each step, who you wanted to be.

I could only

stand on the sidelines,

pointing and cheering and hoping and praying

and clenching my teeth.

And look at you now,

standing strong,

hands outstretched to help the weak.

I wonder

if you can feel my pride,

can sense how much I love you.

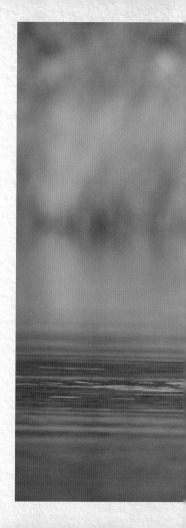

The future is not something we enter.

The future is something we create.

~Leonard Sweet, American author and theologian

You can fail at what you don't want,
so you might as well take a chance
on doing what you love.

———•———

~Jim Carrey, American actor and comedian

He has a destiny only he can fulfill...
because there is greatness within him.

Boys may be made of snails
and puppy dog tails,
but sons are made of
dreams and pride
and expectations and
frustrations
and hugs and a
lifetime of love.

Asking me to describe my son is like
asking me to hold the ocean in a paper cup.

~Jodi Picoult, American novelist

Son, I love you. That's never at stake.

Never, never, never at stake.

———•———

~Kirk Cameron, American actor and producer

Sticky fingers, grassy knees,
secret spy, climbing trees.
Building forts, bugs in jars,
Lego cities, pirate garb.

In a blink, all your toys
turned to peach fuzz
and deltoids;
another blink—a man then—
and my son became my friend.

If someone were to ask me
what has been my biggest accomplishment in life,
I would lift my head high and speak from my heart
with a parent's pride as I said the words
"my son."

~Andrea Adaire Fischer